The Merthyr, Tredegar & Abergavenny Railway

Chris Barber

Amberley

Acknowledgements

I am indebted to members of the Abergavenny Steam Society, who have allowed me to use pictures of the MTA Railway that they have collected over many years. The following members are credited, and their initials are shown with the captions of their pictures: Stan Brown (SB); Gerald Davies (GD); Nigel Lewis (NL); and Pete Sutton (PS). I have also included pictures from the collection of the late Albert Lyons (AL). My own present-day pictures are indicated by the initials (CB). Gerald Davies is given a special thanks for his permission to extract material from Bill Tasker's excellent book *The Merthyr Tredegar & Abergavenny Railway,* which was published in 1986 and is now a collector's item. Gerald knew the author well and inherited the copyright on his death. I also give warm thanks to the Society Chairman, Pete Sutton, and the above members for their advice, which I sought in order to ensure that I did not make mistakes in the telling of this fascinating story. I am also grateful to my wife, Anne Marie, for reading my manuscript and suggesting various improvements.

First published 2017

Amberley Publishing
The Hill, Stroud
Gloucestershire, GL5 4EP

www.amberley-books.com

British Library Cataloguing in Publication Data.
A catalogue record for this book is available from the British Library.

ISBN 978 1 4456 6328 9 (print)
ISBN 978 1 4456 6329 6 (ebook)

Typeset in 9.5pt on 12.5pt Sabon.
Origination by Amberley Publishing.
Printed in the UK.

Contents

Abbreviations Used in the Text

MTA	Merthyr, Tredegar & Abergavenny Railway
LNWR	London & North Western Railway
LMSR	London, Midland & Scottish Railway
BMR	Brecon & Merthyr Railway
GWR	Great Western Railway
TVR	Taff Vale Railway
RR	Rhymney Railway
SLS	Stephenson Locomotive Society

INTRODUCTION

The Merthyr, Tredegar & Abergavenny Railway was one of the most spectacular railways in Britain. However, it was also one of the most difficult to build and one of the most expensive to operate, as it was one of the most severely graded railways in the British Isles, with a 3-mile section of 1 in 34.

It was Crawshay Bailey, the famous ironmaster, who had the drive and energy to make it actually happen, by casting aside strong doubts that such a railway would even be possible; doubts that existed due to the severe gradients and other difficulties that would be involved in creating a route between Abergavenny and Merthyr Tydfil.

John Gardner was the skilled engineer who built the line up through the Clydach Gorge, and its construction was a remarkable engineering achievement. This section was particularly dramatic, with the line twisting and turning, but climbing steadily along a ledge cut into steep slopes above the deep valley.

People from Abergavenny remember this railway with much nostalgia, for it was a time when the town was alive with a symphony of very distinctive sounds, such as the clang of hammers, the hiss of steam, whistles tooting and wheels clattering over joints and points. It also provided considerable employment and, when railway activity in Abergavenny reached its peak, there were over 1,000 people employed in jobs associated with it.

On Tuesdays the trains were always packed with passengers, for this was market day in Abergavenny. Most of the people who lived in farms and smallholdings close to the line used the trains to transport their produce for sale in Abergavenny Market, and as a result the railway company usually had to put on at least one additional train on the line to accommodate the market-day travellers.

It could be a magical experience to travel on the line when the autumn mists had settled in the Usk Valley, and as the Merthyr-bound train climbed up through the Clydach Gorge it would gradually emerge into clear blue skies and sunshine. Looking back towards Abergavenny you would see a sea of cloud with Skirrid Fawr and Sugar Loaf sticking up like rocks in an ocean.

But to travel on the line in winter could be a worrying undertaking, particularly if you were going beyond Brynmawr, for snow at that altitude could bring considerable problems. At Christmas in 1927, at least fourteen locomotives were snowbound at various points along the line between Brynmawr and Merthyr. Forty passengers on one of these trains were marooned for twelve hours at Nantybwch, 1,165 feet above sea level!

Most people who travelled on this railway would remember it mainly as a passenger line, but it should be remembered that it was primarily constructed to pass through the rich mineral measures, which contained all the ingredients required for ironmaking: coal, limestone and ironstone. Not surprisingly, this area along the heads of the industrial valleys is often referred to as the 'Iron Belt'.

The historic market town of Abergavenny was once an important railway centre with three stations: the Great Western on the north to west line, situated to the south-west of the town; Brecon Road, on the former LNWR Abergavenny to Merthyr line; and Abergavenny Junction at the point where the two lines met, north-east of the town. Only the old Great Western station has survived and is still in use.

After the First World War, the 200 railway companies in the UK were consolidated into just four, and on 1 January 1923, the LNWR, along with several other companies, ceased to exist, having been taken over by the London, Midland & Scottish Railway.

By the late 1950s, goods traffic and passenger use had declined as a result of an increase in the number of lorries and bus services, and a steady growth in car ownership. It was a sad day when the line closed in January 1958, but this might not have happened if more people had been using the train.

In Britain there are now nearly 100 preserved railways, many of which operate steam trains. The first in the world was Talyllyn Railway, which was re-opened in 1950 by steam enthusiasts. It is a great shame that the section of the MTA Railway from Abergavenny to Brynmawr was not preserved, for if it was still operating today it would undoubtedly be a popular tourist attraction. At least the route can still be enjoyed by cyclists and walkers.

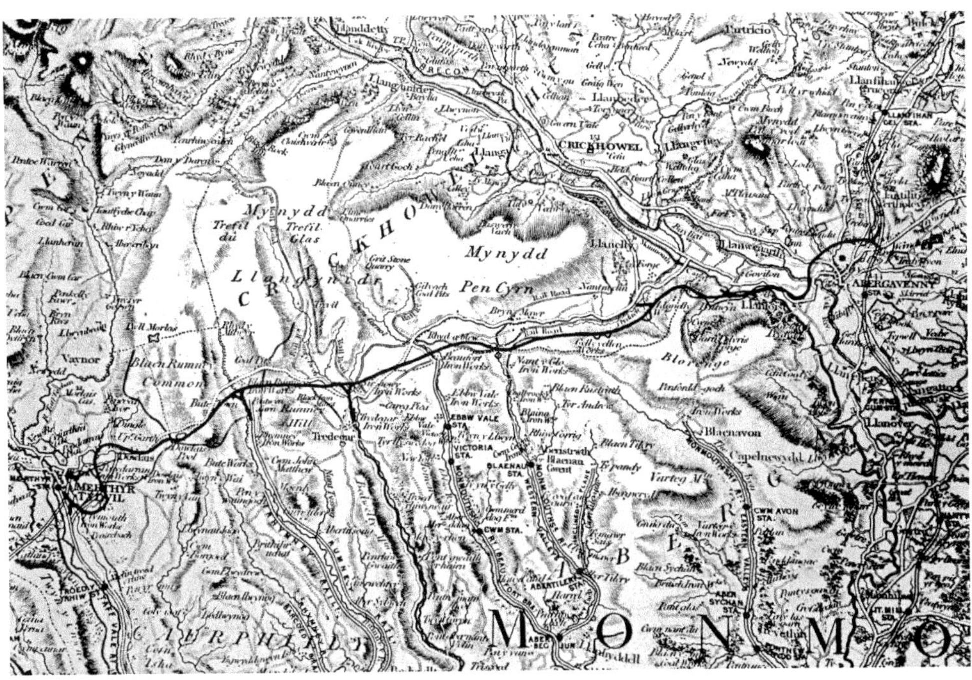

The 24-mile route of the Merthyr, Tredegar & Abergavenny Railway.

1

HOW IT ALL BEGAN

The Llanvihangel Tramroad

The first railroad through Abergavenny was constructed in 1811 for the purpose of conveying coal and lime from the canal at Govilon Wharf towards Hereford. An Act was passed 'for making a railroad from the Brecknock & Abergavenny Canal in the parish of Llanwenarth to or near Llanvihangel Crucorney', and by this Act the proprietors were enabled to form the Llanvihangel Railway Company.

The engineer was John Hodgkinson of Cheltenham and the first section to be constructed ran from Govilon Wharf on the Brecknock & Abergavenny Canal to Llanfoist and then across the River Usk on a stone bridge, which was built alongside the old highway bridge on its western side. The tramroad then continued round to the north of the town, passing close to the New Inn at Mardy and the churches of Llantilio Pertholey and Llanvihangel Crucorney, to end in a field just east of the latter. The total distance was just under 8 miles. Private sidings ran from the tramroad to the limeworks at Llanfoist, to the gasworks at Abergavenny (for the conveyance of coal) and to Triley Mill, near Llantilio Pertholey.

The tramroad bridge built alongside the river bridge at Llanfoist was later replaced by a railway viaduct.

A surviving section of the Llanfihangel railroad near Pandy. (CB)

In 1812, the second section – 5.5 miles in length and known as the Grosmont Tramroad – was constructed. It ran from Llanvihangel Crucorney, following the natural contour of the ground in a westerly direction for about 1 mile. Its route then followed the line of the present-day A465 and finished at Monmouth Cap, near Pontrilas. The final section, called the Hereford Tramroad, which ran from Monmouth Cap to Hereford, was not built until November 1825 due to organised opposition from barge owners and other vested interests.

On Monday, 21 September 1829 at 10 a.m., the final section of the tramroad connecting Govilon Wharf with Hereford was opened for traffic, and the first consignment of coal from Abergavenny arrived at the Wyebridge Wharf. During that day a total of thirty-four trams arrived at the wharf and Thomas Hill, the Blaenavon ironmaster and a generous man, gave orders for ten tons of coal to be distributed among the poor of Hereford.

Crawshay Bailey's Tramroad

In 1820 the construction of a tramroad was authorised, running from the Bailey brothers' ironworks at Nantyglo, through Brynmawr and down the right-hand side of the Clydach Gorge to Govilon Wharf on the Brecknock & Abergavenny Canal. Work started on 6 May 1820 and it must have been a very difficult and costly undertaking. The route was about 5 miles long and the section across the side of Llanelly Hill had to be blasted through high rockfaces.

This twin-track plateway of 4 feet 6 inches gauge was completed on 7 December 1821, which was a remarkable achievement in such a short time. The opening ceremony was celebrated by a line of horse-drawn trams containing 26 tons of coal and 40 tons of bar iron being brought down from Brynmawr. They moved off, preceded by a party in trams specially fitted out for the occasion and a band playing rousing music. Cheers from crowds lining the route welcomed the procession.

In Abergavenny, the bells were rung all day and hundreds of local people greeted the arrival of the coal, which was distributed to the poor and no doubt proved a great source of comfort that winter.

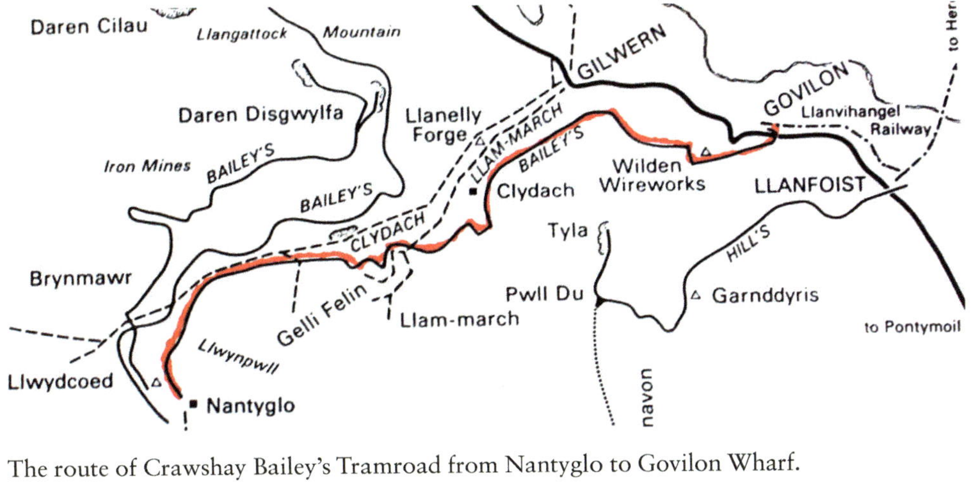

The route of Crawshay Bailey's Tramroad from Nantyglo to Govilon Wharf.

That evening a celebration dinner was held in the Greyhound Hotel, Abergavenny. Toasts were made to the King, the Church, the Lord Lieutenant, the Member of Parliament for Monmouthshire, ironmasters Joseph Bailey, Crawshay Bailey and Thomas Hill, and many other important people who were present.

This tramroad had two purposes – trams loaded with limestone from quarries in the Clydach Gorge were hauled up the gorge to Nantyglo, and, on the return journey, the trams carried iron from the works and coal from the local levels.

The Bailey brothers erected a three-storey warehouse at Govilon Wharf, which was conveniently positioned at the end of their tramroad and the start of the Llanvihangel Tramroad. It was used to store iron that had been produced at their Nantyglo works. Unfortunately, no physical connection between the two tramroads was possible due to the fact that there was a difference in gauges of nearly a foot. This meant that all transference of heavy iron had to be carried out manually.

The Llanvihangel Tramroad ran successfully for the best part of twenty years. However, in 1845 a new company was formed to construct a steam railway from Pontypool to Hereford, and negotiations began with the purpose of acquiring the three tramroads operating between Abergavenny and Hereford.

This three-storey warehouse at Govilon Wharf on the Monmouthshire & Brecon Canal was built by Crawshay Bailey at the Govilon end of his tramroad for storing iron that was brought down from his works at Nantyglo. The iron products were loaded onto narrowboats to be taken down the canal to Newport Docks for export. This building has been restored and now serves as a regional office for the Canals & Rivers Trust. (CB)

The Newport, Abergavenny & Hereford Railway

In 1846, an Act was passed for a Newport, Abergavenny & Hereford Railway, which would have included six branch lines to Panteg, Llangeview, Llanbadoc, Raglan, Abergavenny Gas Works and Portfields in Hereford, but none of these were constructed.

The Company had a capital of £733,000 in £25 shares and the contract was given to James Rennie of Newport. The new line, from its junction with the Monmouthshire Railway at Coedygric to Barton station, Hereford, was opened on 2 January 1854, and on that day Abergavenny received its first train, which clanked its way down 'the bank' from Llanvihangel and came to a squeaky stop at the new station.

On 1 July 1860, the Abergavenny & Hereford Railway Company was taken over by West Midland Co., who in turn were swallowed up by the Great Western Railway on 1 August 1865.

With industry growing in the Monmouthshire Valleys, a railway was urgently needed to link industrial sites between Brynmawr and Merthyr Tydfil, and through Hereford to the Midlands.

In Abergavenny, people were very excited about the proposal that a railway should be built to connect the town with Merthyr Tydfil, and an extract from *The Merlin & Silurian* for 30 January 1858 reads as follows:

> Hope begins to cheer the hearts of the good folk of this town. The brightening prospect of Rail communication between Merthyr and Abergavenny tells its tale upon the spirit of the inhabitants. They are anxious to obtain so desirable an object, as they imagine it will revive the sinking fortunes of what was once one of the most flourishing and best business Towns in the principality, and we are going into the matter with all the ardour and energy of men, who, if they cannot command, will deserve success.

Abergavenny's first station at Monmouth Road. (SB).

2

The Merthyr, Tredegar & Abergavenny Railway

The Act for building the Merthyr, Tredegar & Abergavenny Railway was passed on 1 August 1859 and the specified completion date was to be within five years. Finance was provided through the sale of shares, to give an initial working capital of £150,000, with 7,500 shares of £20 per share. The Act specified a completion day within five years.

The scheme was backed by Crawshay Bailey of Nantyglo, James Hill of Blaenavon and Thomas Brown of Ebbw Vale. By this time, Crawshay Bailey was in sole command of the Nantyglo Ironworks, as his brother Joseph had retired from the business.

A meeting of the proposed company was held on 6 September 1858 at the Angel Hotel, Abergavenny. Several important tradesmen of the town were present, as well as railway engineers Henry Conybeare and John Gardner.

Crawshay Bailey was appointed chairman of the company and he put considerable energy into the enterprise. Strong doubts had been expressed concerning the possibility

Cross Street, Abergavenny, in the days of horse-drawn transport.

of building a railway on so severe a gradient between Llanfoist and Brynmawr; however, Crawshay insisted that, in his opinion, the severest gradient likely to occur on the proposed line would be 1 in 40, and this would be perfectly workable within the estimated cost of £10,000 per mile.

The members of the company were as follows:

Directors:
Crawshay Bailey Esq., MP, Aberaman Park, Glamorganshire
James Hill Esq., Llanwenarth House, Monmouthshire
John Jayne Esq., Pant-y-Bailey House, Llanelly, Breconshire
Edward Charles Strode Esq., South Hill House, Somerset
Henry Thomas Esq., Lwyn Madoc, Breconshire
Chairman of the Quarter Sessions, Glamorganshire

Secretary:
A. T. Gordon Esq.

Engineers:
Messrs Birkenshaw & Conybeare, 22 Abingdon St., London
John Gardner Esq., 18 Adam St., London

Solicitor:
S. F. Noyes Esq., 5 Lincoln's-Inn-Fields, London

Local Solicitors:
W. F. Batt Esq., Abergavenny
Messrs Morgan & Smith, Merthyr and Aberdare
R. Waters Esq., Tredegar

Bankers:
Messrs Masterman & Co., 35 Nicholas Lane, London
Messrs Bailey, Williams & Co.
West of England & South Wales District Bank, Tredegar
Messrs Wilkins & Co., Merthyr

Brokers:
Messrs R. & J. Sutton, 22 Royal Exchange, London

The temporary offices were at 18 Adam Street, Adelphi, London, and 'applications for prospectuses and shares [were] to be made to the secretary, brokers or local solicitors'.

The first meeting of the provisional directors and promoters was held on 15 November 1858 under Crawshay Bailey's chairmanship in Abergavenny Town Hall. The following year, on 1 August, the enabling Act received its Royal Assent, but due to a lack of financial support from the Merthyr area it was initially decided to concentrate on building the line only as far as Nantybwch.

Crawshay Bailey

Crawshay Bailey was born on 24 October 1789, the younger son of John Bailey of Wakefield, Yorkshire, and Susannah Crawshay, the sister of Richard Crawshay, who owned the Cyfarthfa Ironworks at Merthyr Tydfil. At the age of twelve, Crawshay left his native Yorkshire and came to Merthyr to join his older brother Joseph in learning the iron trade in the employment of their uncle.

When Richard Crawshay died in 1810, he bequeathed a quarter share of the Cyfarthfa Ironworks to Joseph, then aged twenty-seven, and £1,000 to Crawshay, aged twenty-one. Richard Crawshay's son-in-law, Benjamin Hall, was sole executor and the large legacies left to Crawshay and Joseph enabled them to purchase Nantyglo Ironworks.

Crawshay continued to work at Cyfarthfa until 1820, when he joined his brother Joseph at Nantyglo on the departure of his partner, Matthew Wayne. Together the two brothers made Nantyglo Ironworks one of the greatest in the world. They also bought Beaufort Works, and the two ironworks were run as one concern.

A nineteenth-century engraving of Nantyglo Ironworks, where seven blast furnaces produced 70,000 tons of iron a year. It was regarded as one of the most important ironworks in the world at that time.

The Bailey brothers were also responsible for the rebuilding of Nantyglo House and Crawshay lived there until 1860. By then he had amassed a fortune and had purchased large areas of land at Aberaman, Mountain Ash and the Rhondda Valleys. In buying the Aberaman estate in 1836 he also took possession of its mansion.

Joseph retired from the management of the Nantyglo Ironworks in 1830 and moved to Glan Usk Estate, near Crickhowell, in 1830. Here, he spent the rest of his life with his second wife, Mary Ann Hooper. He was made a baronet in 1852 and died six years later.

In 1820 Crawshay had married Ann Moore of Surrey, who failed to provide him with a male heir, but Sarah Baker, a servant in the household, bore him a son in 1841 – Crawshay Bailey Jnr.

In 1821, Crawshay was responsible for the construction of a tramway from Beaufort and Nantyglo down the Clydach Gorge to Llanfoist to join the Brecon & Abergavenny Canal. In 1837 he was appointed High Sheriff of Brecknock and of Monmouthshire in 1851. Between 1852 and 1868 he was the Conservative MP for the Monmouthshire boroughs, which included Newport, and, having fought five successful elections, he was eventually defeated by Sir John Ramsden.

Llanfoist House was the home of Crawshay Bailey, and as chairman of the MTA Company he was obviously privileged as, when the line was completed, passenger trains used to stop opposite the lodge gates to pick him up or set him down when travelling to and from Nantyglo. His valet would assist the elderly gent down the steps that had been specially erected for his convenience.

He was a great promoter of railways, which helped to swell his fortune with the increase in demand for iron rails. In 1845, he and Sir Josiah John Guest obtained a Parliamentary Act to connect the Aberdare Railway with the Taff Vale Railway at Abercynon. Then, in 1852, he promoted a railway from the Forest of Dean via Coleford, Monmouth and Usk to Pontypool.

Crawshay retired from Nantyglo in 1845 and left the management of the works in the hands of his nephew, William Partridge. He bought Llanfoist House and retired there in 1850, having worked hard for nearly seventy-five years. Of all the ironmasters he is probably the most famous, and, living to the age of eighty-two, he died on 9 January 1872.

Construction of the Railway between Abergavenny and Brynmawr

In 1859, the MTA Company purchased the Bailey Tramroad for the sum of £20,000. Crawshay Bailey took £15,000 in shares and Thomas Brown of Ebbw Vale, subject to an agreement dated 1 February 1859, took £5,000.

A contract was entered into with William McCormick Esq. MP, for the construction of the railway from Abergavenny to Brynmawr. On Monday, 18 June 1860, the ceremony of turning the first sod was performed in pouring rain by Mrs Crawshay Bailey at the site of the intended station on the Brecon Road.

Mr Charles Daniel, the Chairman of the Ceremonial Committee, made a speech, stating that it was a great pleasure to be the mouthpiece of the committee, and reading an address of acknowledgement to Mrs Bailey from the shareholders and promoters of the undertaking. He obviously had a sense of humour, for it included the following words:

> It now, Madam, becomes our pleasant duty to do formally and publicly what we have already done in a more private capacity, namely, to invite you to a proof of your dexterity in the use of an implement that seldom passes through a lady's hands, and thus to show to the stalwart sons of toil around you, and to others, who are not so familiar with the spade, the way to employ the symbol of Industry and harbinger of civilisation.

This was followed by loud cheers and then Mr John Gardner, who had been appointed Chief Engineer, presented Mrs Crawshay Bailey with the ceremonial silver spade and commented that she was very kind in agreeing to perform the ceremony. She raised the turf with considerable difficulty, as it had been consolidated by heavy rain and also much trampled by people, but she managed to raise a piece of turf and deposit it in a wheelbarrow, which she wheeled along a plank before tipping it out. The spade used was made of silver and polished oak by Messrs Hayne & Carter of Red Lion Street, Clerkenwell, London. It bore the following inscription: 'With this spade the first sod of the MTA. Rly was turned by Mrs Crawshay Bailey, on the 18th of June 1860.'

The shops in Abergavenny were closed and flags and banners were displayed at various places, while church bells rang almost continuously all day.

There then followed a series of engineer's reports on the progress made. The first one, dated 27 August 1860, was most favourable:

> Since the commencement of the works in June by the contractor, Mr McCormick, considerable progress has been made with the bridges and other works, between Abergavenny and Brynmawr. Eight bridges are now in the course of erection, several of which are nearly completed. The Tramroad Viaduct over the Usk has been pulled down and the foundations for the new structure commenced. The earthworks at the faces of both tunnels are in progress (Clydach 330 yards and Gelli Felin 352 yards). The bridges are being built for a double line, but only one set of rails will be laid down. The underbridges are being made for a single line only, and the tunnels are also for single line.

On 19 August 1861 at the general half-yearly meeting, held at the company's office in Monk Street, Abergavenny, the engineer, John Gardner, reported on further progress and optimistically saw no difficulty in completing the line as far as Brynmawr, which would be open for traffic within six or seven months.

By this time the tunnels were well advanced, with about half the length completed and both tunnels being expected to be finished in less than six months. Excellent progress had also been made on the bridges and viaducts, with twenty-seven out of thirty being either finished, or nearly so. The earthworks for the stations at Abergavenny and Brynmawr had also been commenced, and plans for the station buildings were to be ready shortly.

The London & North Western Railway Company Take Control

Ever-increasing costs of building this railway over such difficult country resulted in the MTA Company's account becoming overdrawn in the latter part of 1861, and the London & North Western Railway Company (LNWR) agreed to take control of the project with a 1,000-year lease.

The LNWR had been formed in 1846 by the merger of the Grand Junction Railway, the London & Birmingham Railway and the Manchester & Birmingham Railway, and in 1862 it absorbed the MTA Railway as well.

This portion of the LNWR was completely isolated from its parent system, and when the MTA came into operation it could only be reached by the gracious permission of the Great Western Railway (GWR), who very kindly allowed the LNWR to use the 23 miles of their line between Red Hill Junction, near Hereford, and Abergavenny Junction (the old Newport, Abergavenny & Hereford Railway), where the MTA line branched off to the South West.

In just two years this first section of the line from Abergavenny to Brynmawr was completed and it was opened on 29 September 1862. A new iron bridge had been built over the River Usk and a long embankment had been constructed between the canal and the river. Seven more bridges had to be built between Llanfoist and Brynmawr, as well as two tunnels, each about a quarter of a mile in length, and long stretches of stone retaining walls. This was one of the most severely graded railways in the British Isles, with a 3-mile section of 1 in 34. When the trains reached Brynmawr it was necessary for them to take on additional water, having climbed no less than 1,000 feet to the highest town in Wales.

A postcard depicting the road bridge and iron railway viaduct spanning the River Usk.

The Official Opening of the Section from Abergavenny to Brynmawr

Colonel Yolland, the Government Inspector of Railways, checked the line from the junction to Brynmawr on Thursday, 18 September 1862. He passed it without it requiring the slightest alteration or addition, and expressed his full satisfaction with everything he had seen.

The opening of this first section of the railway (a distance of about 9 miles) took place eleven days later, on Monday, 29 September 1862, and it was celebrated in the two towns with tremendous enthusiasm. A procession formed at the Angel Hotel and included the directors, the chief engineer and his assistants, contractors, shareholders, tradesmen and the Monmouthshire Militia Band. They proceeded on foot to Brecon Road, where the MTA station had been gaily decorated with flowers and evergreens, as had the nearby Railway Inn.

Several speeches were made, including one by Crawshay Bailey, who commented:

> In the year 1811, I had no idea that we should have a railway here now. When we first came to Nantyglo to carry on the Works we found that in the parish of Llanelly – now called Brynmawr – there was only one Farm House, only one single house. Now there is a population of 7,000, beating, I believe, the County Town and not only have we that number of inhabitants at Brynmawr, but in the parish of Aberystruth, where we are now standing, there is a population of about 15,000. I think we may take that as a tolerably good earnest that the L&NW Railway Company will have some little traffic down the line (hear, hear).
>
> We are all interested in the iron trade; and if we push on to Tredegar we shall get into another large population there and in the Ebbw Valley. Then again, there is another heavy population at Rhymney; and if we get on towards Merthyr and

Aberdare, we shall have a population of about 150,000 inhabitants, and if that won't give a passenger trade, I don't know what will (cheers). Down in the Western Valleys we used to have a sort of rumble-tumble coach which went at a rate of about 4 miles an hour on the old tramroad. Now we have our locomotive trains on that line and the Monmouthshire Company are in receipt of from £18,000 to £20,000 a year from passenger traffic.

Mr George Finlay, one of the directors of the MTA Railway, then commented that it was only within the last few months that he had the honour of a connection with the LNWR, but he had been, for some years, connected with the trade of South Wales. He was quite sure that the LNWR, in taking a lease of the MTA line, had acted on a right and safe policy. On the occasion of his first journey over the railway, he never saw a line more substantially constructed or one better adapted for carrying on the enormous traffic that lay before them. The LNWR had only as recently as the day before appeared in that district, but for many years past they had carried on an enormous trade in connection with it.

Three cheers for the directors were called for and there was a hearty response. A train of six carriages and a powerful engine then moved forward. In a very short time every seat was occupied, and in many instances nine or ten persons were crowded into spaces usually allotted to half a dozen.

The signal for starting was given and at about 10.30 a.m. a canon was fired. Amid loud cheers from the assembled spectators, the train began the journey to Brynmawr.

The train was driven as far as Govilon by Mrs Hill, the wife of Captain Hill, the vice-chairman of the company, under the direction of John Gardner, the engineer. The driver obeyed the injunctions from the company chairman and the train moved along at a very slow and steady pace.

When the train arrived at Brynmawr station, there were loud cheers as Crawshay Bailey stepped off the train, for this was his home ground and his Nantyglo Works provided employment for thousands of people in the locality. He received a tremendous welcome and members of the Brynmawr Local Board of Health showed their appreciation.

An address was read by Mr Cox Davies of Llangrwyney House, the clerk to the Board:

To C rawshay Bailey, Esquire, mp, the Chairman
J. G. Hill, Esquire, Deputy Chairman
Thomas Brown, JohnJjayne, E. C. Stroude, and Isaac Isaacs Esquires

The directors of the Merthyr, Tredegar and Abergavenny Railway Company

We, the undersigned members of the Brynmawr local board of health,on behalf of ourselves and other shareholders in the company, and inhabitants of Brynmawr and its neighbourhood, beg you to accept our hearty congratulations on your arrival at this station for the purpose of opening the first section of the line from Abergavenny to Merthyr.

We recall with pride the energetic efforts made by all classes at all places along the line successfully to launch this scheme at its inception in 1858.

We recall with gratitude and satisfaction the sagacious and unwearying attention by yourselves and the officers of the company upon their affairs and the gratifying success in which your efforts have resulted.

We regard the opening of this line as the commencement of a new era for the hill districts on the borders of Monmouthshire and Brecknockshire.

We hope to see the agricultural wealth of many a lowland vale, powered forth along this line to supply the necessities of these mining populations, and returned by abundant supplies of the inexhaustible mineral treasures here produced.

We anticipate the time when this and other improved facilities of the inexhaustible mineral treasures here produced.

We anticipate the time when this and other improved facilities of communication shall lead to the establishment in our district of some of the many more advanced manufacturers in which iron is employed, attracted here by the abundant supply of metal and the cheapness of labour and fuel, and we are sanguine enough to hope that time will find Brynmawr the centre of a system of railways converging upon it from Blaenavon, Blaina and other adjacent districts.

We see such of the slopes of our surrounding hills as cultivation has touched, if incapable of growing corn, yet producing a sward of grass, which for greeness and luxuriance, few valley meadows can surpass, and we hope as work expands with the increased facilities of communication, that greater breadths of this land will be brought under cultivation for the benefit alike of the landowners and the resident populations.

We trust the brightening prospects which seem now dawning, after the long depression of the South Wales iron trade, will ripen into the full daylight of prosperity, and we fervently pray that it will please the almighty disposer of all worldly events, who has made labour the lot of man, to give a long continued and unclouded success to the work which you have this day so far prosperously accomplished.

James Phillips, Chairman

Roger Edwards
George Hicks
Solomon Chilton
Edward Edwards
Thomas Hope

William Thomas
David Morgan
Thomas Kershaw
John Lloyd
James Evans
K. J. Cox Davies, Clerk to the board

Presented at Brynmawr station, upon the opening of the line on Monday the 29th September 1862.

Shortly afterwards, at 12.30 p.m., the directors started on the return journey to Abergavenny. When the train arrived it was greeted with the firing of a cannon and hearty cheers from the large crowd who were still assembled at the station.

A celebratory dinner was held at the Angel Hotel, Abergavenny, with a liberal supply of champagne being supplied by the authorities of the London & North Western

Railway Company. They had given notice earlier that month that they had completed arrangements for the leasing and working of the line and were ready to start at a day's notice, but the Act for transferring all the outstanding estate and interest in the MTA Railway to the LNWR was not completed until 30 July 1866.

A public dinner was also held at the Griffin Hotel, Brynmawr, and was attended by the shareholders and tradesmen of the town. Mr Cox Davies was in the chair. During the afternoon, the children of various Sunday schools had paraded around the town, singing hymns and various songs. After dark, a large fire balloon was sent up and there was also a firework display by Mr Jones, the chemist.

Immediately after the opening of the line, the service consisted of four trains in each direction between Abergavenny and Brynmawr. They were as follows:

Departure from Abergavenny at 8.00 a.m., 10.00 a.m., 10.40 a.m., 7.00 p.m.

Departure from Brynmawr at 9.00 a.m., 12.30 p.m., 1.30 p.m., 8.00 p.m.

In May 1863 the service was adjusted as follows:

Departure from Abergavenny (Brecon Road) at 9.40 a.m., 12.45 p.m., 3.40 p.m. and 6.00 p.m.

Arrival at Brynmawr at 10.20 a.m., 1.25 p.m., 4.20 p.m. and 6.40 p.m.

A road coach for Merthyr connected with the 1.25 p.m. train at Brynmawr, and there were also four trains in the opposite direction. In June 1863 a Sunday service commenced, but this ceased within a year.

At the half-yearly meeting on Thursday, 27 August 1863, the engineer reported that a passenger station had been opened at Gilwern, while a waiting room had also been erected and a platform made at the junction of the MTA line with the West Midland Railway Company. This was later known as the Abergavenny Junction station.

By 1882, some fifty trains a day were operating in each direction between Abergavenny and Brynmawr.

Extension of the Line

On 14 February 1862, McCormick was awarded the contract to build the line to Nantybwch. This 4.25-mile extension was opened on 1 March 1864. It had involved the construction of two viaducts: the 93-yard-long Beaufort Viaduct and the nine-arch, 118-yard-long Blaen y Cwm Viaduct.

Further westward, progress was contested by the Brecon & Merthyr Railway (BMR), which in 1863 had reached Pant. They were planning to reach Merthyr itself and to push eastwards to Rhymney, so they were obviously opposed to the LNWR making further progress towards Merthyr.

In 1864 an agreement was made with the Rhymney Railway Company to jointly construct the 3 miles of track from Nantybwch, through Rhymney Bridge to Rhymney, with the LNWR being given running powers over the Rhymney line to Cardiff Docks.

The section of railway between Brynmawr and Nantybwch was passed as suitable for passenger traffic by the Government Inspector for Railways on 11 February 1864, and officially opened on 1 March.

In 1868 the BMR completed its line round the north and west of Merthyr, and this involved the construction of the Pontsarn and Cefn Coed Viaducts, which spanned the two River Taffs.

Slow progress was made by the LNWR on the next section towards Merthyr, with just another 3 miles of single line being completed between Rhymney Bridge and Ivor Junction. This came into operation on 1 January 1873 under an agreement made on 23 March 1871 between the LNWR and the BMR.

In 1873, the LNWR extended the line westward and opened a passenger station near the BMR at Dowlais Top, 1,250 feet above sea level, where a connection was made with the Brecon & Merthyr Railway.

The LNWR had proposed to reach Merthyr by a route that would overcome the difference of about 400 feet in altitude between Dowlais and Merthyr by means of a spiral approach down the hillside east of the Merthyr. However, the BMR Company agreed to 6 miles of its own Merthyr branch becoming a joint line with the LNWR and on 9 June 1879 the line finally reached Merthyr High Street station.

Opening of the Merthyr Extension Line

On Saturday, 14 June 1879, the *Merthyr Express* reported:

> This new line was opened for traffic on Monday, June the 9th. The first passenger train entered the new section at Penywern Junction about 9.10 am, the engine being decorated with evergreens. The various bridges on the route were crowded with people, who heartily cheered the passing train. Most of the chief officials of the lines interested were present at Merthyr. The LNWR was represented by Mr Bishop, the District Superintendent, Mr Entwistle, his assistant, Mr Gardner, Mr Young, Mr F. Smith, and Mr Serymgeour, the Auditor.

Doubling the Track between Abergavenny and Brynmawr

By 1877 the traffic on the line had increased so much that it was decided to double the track on the section to Brynmawr and the chief engineer, John Gardner, was called upon to oversee the widening of all the railway viaducts, the boring of two extra tunnels and the laying of additional track. This was all completed in a surprisingly short time.

John Gardner had been born on 16 December 1821 and was the son of Harrie Gardner, a civil engineer. After a period of assisting his father, John was appointed as an assistant engineer on the London & Greenwich Railway in about 1840. He was later engaged in a similar capacity at Newport Docks. He designed railway girders for bridges that had a combination of wrought and cast iron for the Reading & Reigate Railway and he started to practice on his own account around 1850.

He acted as engineer for the Staines & Wokingham, the Merthyr, Tredegar & Abergavenny, the Nantwich & Market Drayton, the Ebbw Vale, and the Brynmawr & Blaenavon lines. He also made surveys for projected lines from the Rhondda Valley to Newport and Cardiff, and from Abergavenny to Brecon and to Monmouth.

On 6 May 1851 he was elected an Associate of the Institute of Civil Engineers, and transferred to the class of Member on 8 February 1870.

Due to ill health, Gardner had to retire in 1885. He died nine years later, on 15 January, at the age of seventy-three. His obituary notice carried the citation: 'He was an engineer

John Gardner's name can still be seen on the red sandstone abutment of the railway bridge that he constructed to carry the MT&A line over the River Usk at Llanfoist. (CB)

of ability, upright in all business transactions and esteemed for the conscientious manner in which he carried out the works entrusted to his care.'

The Death of Crawshay Bailey

In 1872, Crawshay Bailey passed away at the age of eighty-two, so unfortunately never saw his dream of building the railway all the way to Merthyr come to fruition. He was succeeded by his only son and heir, Crawshay Bailey Junior (1821–1887) of Maindiff Court.

In Llanfoist churchyard is a conspicuous, tall granite pillar, which marks the site of a vault containing the coffins of Crawshay Bailey and his wife. It attracts lots of visitors, but some are often confused about the connection between the Crawshays of Merthyr and Crawshay Bailey. They mistakenly come to Llanfoist looking for a massive granite slab, bearing the inscription 'God Forgive Me'. It commemorates Robert Thompson Crawshay of Cyfarthfa Castle and can be seen in Vaynor churchyard near Merthyr Tydfil.

Llanfoist Church was restored in 1872 as a memorial to Crawshay Bailey. (CB)

A memorial window to Crawshay Bailey.

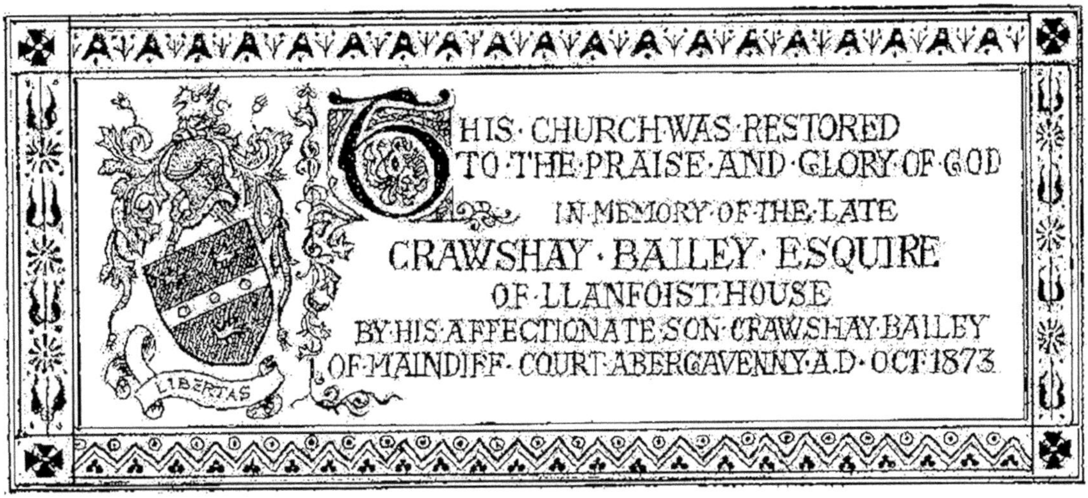

A drawing of the memorial plaque to the ironmaster Crawshay Bailey.

The Funeral of Crawshay Bailey Senior

On 20 January 1872, the *Abergavenny Chronicle* printed the following:

> Although it was announced that the funeral was to be strictly private, between 3,000 and 4,000 people assembled, chiefly composed of those who were connected with the Nantyglo and Beaufort Ironworks, and who, by their demeanour, expressed the sorrow they felt at the death of their late employer. The road was lined from the lodge to the church. The funeral was announced to start at 12 o' clock, but it was about 12.45 before the procession started.
>
> The choir, which consisted of a part of Rehoboth (Independent) Choir, Brynmawr and part of the Wesleyan Choir, Nantyglo upon the march from the house, sang in slow time the 'Old Hundreth'.
>
> After the arrival at the church, which was crowded to excess, the Reverend James Pugh read the prayers and the Reverend G. Howells read the lesson. Before the removal of the body, the united choirs sang Pope's ode of 'Vital Spark' very beautifully and with great expression.
>
> Upon the removal of the body from the church to the vault, the choir sang a most impressive Hymn. The large concourse here assembled, quietly opened and made way for the funeral cortege to pass to the vault. After the body was lowered, the Reverend James Pugh read the last funeral rites.
>
> After the service had been read, Mr Crawshay Bailey Junior and two gentlemen went into the vault and placed a white camelia (the favourite flower of the deceased) upon the coffin.
>
> Many present were afterwards allowed to go into the vault and take a last look at the coffin of the deceased, which was placed in the centre. On the right hand was the mortal remains of the late Mrs Bailey. On the left, that of the late Captain Lewis, and the coffins were apparently in a good state of preservation.

The outer coffin was of polished oak (the inner one being an elm shell and lead coffin) with brass furniture, the plate bearing the following inscription:

CRAWSHAY BAILEY
Died 9th January,
1872
Aged 82

The tenants after the funeral partook of a repast prepared for them at the Greyhound Hotel. Although market day in the town, the various shops were partially closed out of respect for the deceased.

3

Abergavenny, An Important Railway Town

Visitors to Abergavenny are often surprised to learn that this town used to be a very important railway centre with three stations: the GWR at Monmouth Road, the LNWR at the Junction, and Brecon Road on the MTA line. Only Monmouth Road station has survived today and it is still in use with trains running between Cardiff and Crewe. The suffix 'Monmouth Road' was added by British Railways in 1950, but was removed in 1958 as the other two stations had closed.

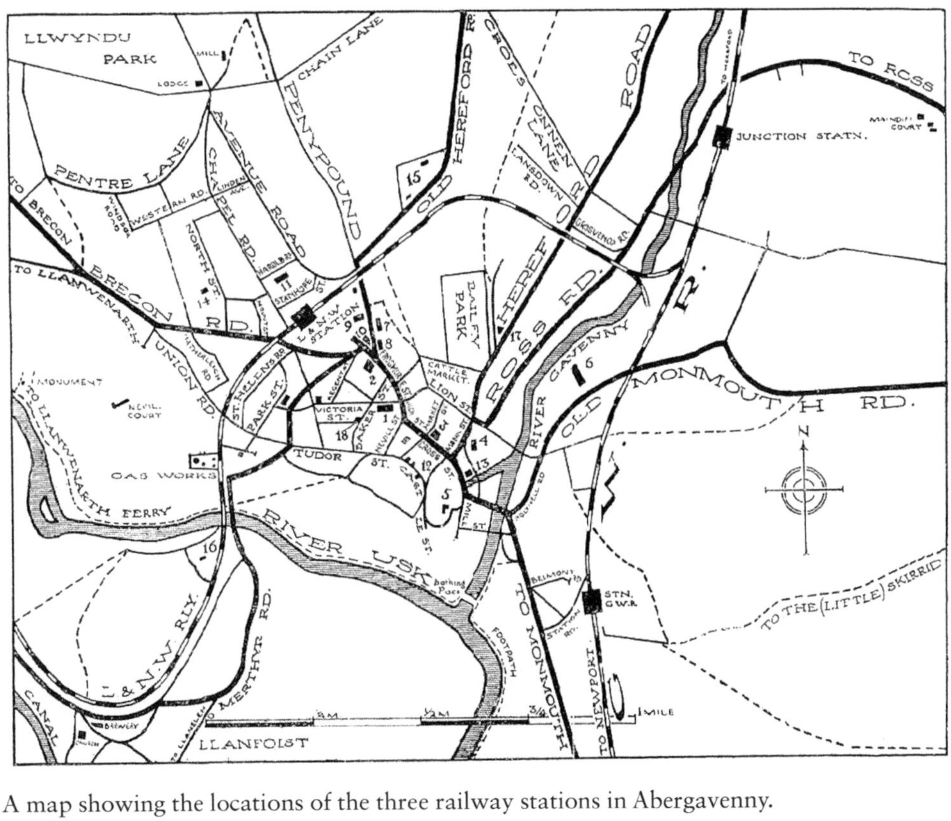

A map showing the locations of the three railway stations in Abergavenny.

Monmouth Road station, situated on the main GWR to Hereford line, remains open today, with trains travelling in each direction between Cardiff and Crewe. (CB)

Brecon Road station (now demolished) was situated on the MTA branch from the Junction to Merthyr. (SB)

Abergavenny Junction station first opened on 1 October 1862 – the first day of the LNWR's lease of the line and the commencement of passenger services. On 20 June 1872 it was re-sited 552 yards further north to improve access to the MTA line. (SB)

The LNWR opened the Union Road Engine Shed in November 1867 and in later years it was enlarged to accommodate about forty-seven engines under cover. There were facilities for maintaining 100 engines and these sheds were a hive of activity 24 hours a day, seven days a week. The staff were continually involved in servicing visiting locomotives as well as their own company engines. (SB)

Interior of the locomotive sheds, *c.* 1956. (NL)

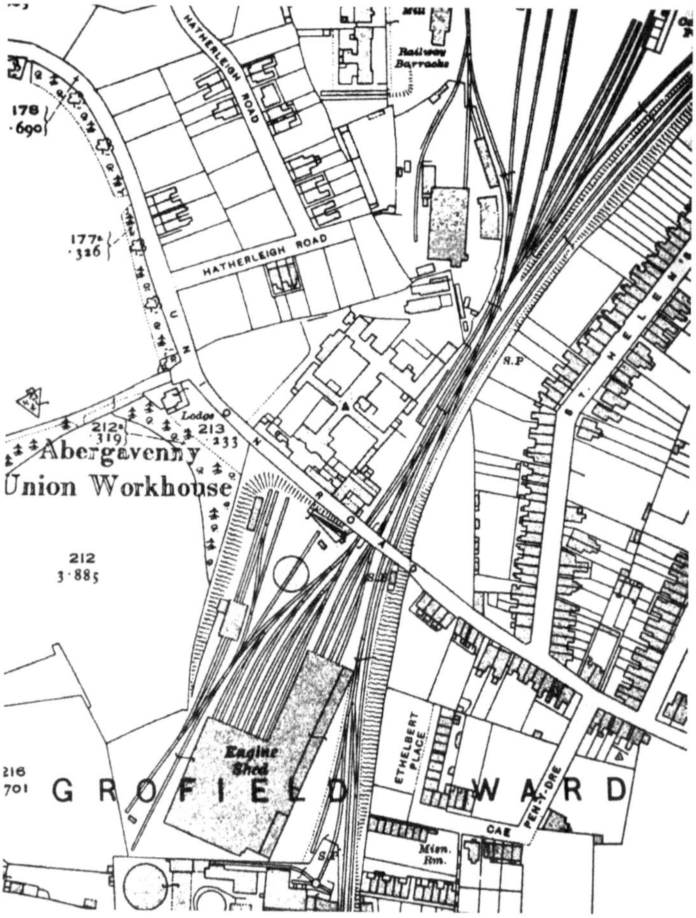

Location of the Engine Shed at Union Road.

To the right of the bridge is the pump house on the Down side of the MTA line. The pump was steam driven until about 1928, when electricity took over. Water was raised from the River Usk to supply Brecon Road, the Junction and Monmouth Road. (NL)

No. 46616 lined up with tank engines Nos 58925, 58915 and 58924 at the loco sheds. (NL)

No. 2620, a 19 in. goods locomotive at Union Road. (SB)

A large turntable measuring 50 feet across was erected in 1899 and was removed in 1953. This locomotive is a reminder that the LNWR was amalgamated into the London, Midland & Scottish Railway (LMS) in the 1923 grouping. (AL)

The LNWR carriage shed at Abergavenny Junction. (SB)

Oiling the lubricators at Union Road sheds in 1953. (SB)

LMS Coal Tank No. 58902 at Union Road in 1953. (SB)

Merthyr train at Brecon Road station. (SB)

A Coal Tank engine on the ash pits at Abergavenny loco sheds in August 1953. In the centre of the picture is the fire-dropping tool rack, with rakes, tongs, pokers, etc. Ashpan cleaning was hard, hot and dirty work. (AL)

The Abergavenny Junction ambulance team were winners of the railway ambulance competition in 1938. The man seated on the left is stationmaster Mr Baker. (AL)

This GWR charabanc was hired for a railwayman's trip to the Wye Valley in 1910. It cost them 1*s* 6*d* each and they must have had a bumpy ride as the vehicle had solid tyres. Another problem was that the wooden brake blocks sometimes caught fire on steep descents. (AL)

The GWR bus service from Abergavenny to Brecon began operating on 1 July 1905. This Milnes-Daimler petrol-engined double-decker bus, with a stairway leading to the upper deck, was capable of carrying fourteen passengers and had a compartment for luggage. The fare to Brecon was 2*s* 6*d*. (AL)

Joseph Bishop was employed as the first superintendent of the Abergavenny, Merthyr & Districts of the London & North Western Railway Company. He had come to Abergavenny in 1864 and was held in such high esteem that when Queen Victoria restored the charter to the borough in 1899, he became the town's first mayor. When he died in 1902 after a short illness at the age of forty-seven, practically the whole of Abergavenny was in mourning, as he was a very popular man who had given twenty-five years of service to the town. For many years the mayors and councillors of Abergavenny were railway officials and even the first Co-operative store was started by a railway company. (GD)

This picture, taken at Brecon Road signal box No. 1 in 1920, shows the *Engineer South Wales*, which had been built in Crewe in 1852. It was used by the district engineer of the LNWR who had his headquarters at Brecon Road station and used this engine and a single coach as a mobile inspection office. (AL)

To make sure the railwaymen of the day could live near their jobs, the authorities built houses for them in nearby streets. The present Cantref Inn was the first new building to spring up in the area, even before Brecon Road station. After that came the houses in Stanhope Street, North Street and St Helen's Road, followed by an influx of railwaymen to occupy them.

A bell hung in the station yard tolled to bring the men running to their jobs on time. It was also used to signal finishing time, and is now in Abergavenny Museum.

The Railway Inn on Brecon Road was formerly known as the White Hart, but in 1865 the name was changed to the Railway Hotel, and later on it became the Railway Inn. (CB)

A party of railwaymen assembled outside the Somerset Inn on Merthyr Road in 1912, before departing on a charabanc outing. In 1901 this pub had become the headquarters of the Abergavenny branch of the Amalgamated Society of Railway Servants. (AL)

The Central Office at Brecon Road station was built in 1867. In this 1911 photograph, the messenger boys are awaiting their delivery notes. (AL)

Some of the staff of the Abergavenny locomotive department posing for a photograph in front of No. 2525, outside the shed building, in around 1900. (NL)

The cleaners worked in teams of five and they could generally produce a spick and span locomotive in around two hours. To work your way up from cleaner to engine driver would have taken a very long time. One could work for up to five years as a cleaner, then twelve years or so as a fireman, before starting training for the top job at the age of at least thirty-five. (AL)

Some workers take a rest from loading tons of coal at Abergavenny loco sheds in the late 1940s. (AL)

A group of young firemen and cleaners enjoying a break at the loco sheds. Their work was often hard and involved long hours. Railwaymen were also poorly paid. A signalman, for example, was paid as little as 17*s* 6*d* a week in 1900, and on occasions he worked for twelve to eighteen hours at a stretch. (AL)

Comradeship among railway workers was strong: here is a cheerful group of the Abergavenny loco sheds' football team in 1949. (AL)

LMS staff serving the MTA line in 1923, but it is interesting that the second man on the left in the second row still wears an LNWR hat. (AL)

This party of loco shed men went to London to see the railway sports at the Crystal Palace in the 1920s. The wreath was to be laid at the cenotaph. (AL)

Members of the local breakdown gang who came to the rescue of locomotive No. 6963, which was derailed at Monmouth Road in the early 1950s. (AL)

Platelayers maintaining the sidings near offices at the loco sheds in 1947. (AL)

Jack Hinkley oiling points at the loco sheds in 1946. This proud railwayman took his job very seriously. (AL)

4

Abergavenny Junction to Merthyr High Street

Abergavenny Junction station was situated on a GWR line and was opened by the LNWR specifically to cater for passengers travelling on their Merthyr line. This was where the MTA and the GWR lines met and the passengers who boarded here were mainly those changing trains. (NL)

A train at Abergavenny Junction having returned from Merthyr. (GD)

Engine No. 4955 *Plas Power Hall* seen in September 1952. (NL)

The large carriage shed on the left was added in the 1920s. (SB)

The unique GWR/LMS signal box was situated on a Great Western Line and was operated by GWR staff. In 1965 the box was replaced by a ground frame further south. (NL)

Gravestone of an Abergavenny Junction stationmaster in Abergavenny cemetery. (CB)

The footbridge was dismantled when the MTA line closed in 1958 and it was re-erected at Monmouth Road station. (GD)

A train arriving at Abergavenny Junction. (GD)

The three-arched bridge taking the line over Tredillion Road with Great Western pannier tank No. 4630 in the distance, which was photographed in 1956. (SB)

Engine No. 6427 passing below Grosvernor Road, December 1947. (NL)

The line crosses the Old Hereford Road on this short bridge. To the right can be seen a toll house, providing a reminder of the days when traders had to pay a toll when entering Abergavenny by any of its roads. (AL)

Brecon Road station. (AL)

The 5.05 p.m. passenger train to Merthyr is about to depart from Brecon Road station, drawn by engine No. 40145. (AL)

A LNWR 0-8-4 leaving Brecon Road station with a train for Merthyr. It would give a shrill whistle and then cross the Brecon Turnpike Road on an iron girder bridge. (NL)

The bridge over Brecon Road was demolished in 1977. (AL)

The MTA line passed under the Union Road bridge through the arch on the right. Beside it is No. 2 signal box, which controlled the trains to and from Merthyr, as well as the locomotive sheds and workshops. (NL)

The construction of a link road from the river bridge to the A40 Brecon Road in the 1970s has covered what remained of the locomotive sheds and workshops, and the stone bridge has been replaced by a footbridge. (CB)

A Merthyr-bound train crossing the Llanfoist Viaduct. (NL)

A freight train crossing the viaduct towards Brecon Road station. (NL)

Looking back towards Brecon Road station. (AL)

Looking along the track bed towards Llanfoist. (NL)

The line reaches the village of Llanfoist with Blorenge mountain looming in the distance. (NL)

This row of cottages, known as Casaba Terrace, was built in 1878 to house railway workers and their families. (CB)

The origin of the name Casaba is not known and it is strange that the letter 'S' is back to front.

The old Llanfoist Inn (now called the 'Spice Lounge'), with Blorenge mountain in the background. The railway ran to the right of the red car. (CB)

A photograph taken from the Monmouthshire & Brecon Canal in around 1890, showing the double track passing behind houses in The Cutting, Llanfoist.

Skew Bridge, which spans the Merthyr Road just west of Llanfoist, was built to carry the MTA line. It was constructed by the founder of Robert Price & Sons, the Abergavenny builders merchants who owned local stone quarries. Robert Price was known as 'Price the Cutter'. (CB)

A 0-8-0 'Super D' pulling a mixed train in 1938 and struggling up this long embankment from Llanfoist, which begins at 1 in 70 and then steepens to 1 in 40, followed by a gradient of 1 in 34. (NL)

At the end of Govilon Wharf the line crossed the canal on another skew bridge, which is an impressive structure. (CB)

If you stand on the towpath and look up at the brickwork you can see how the bridge was widened when the track was doubled in 1877. (CB)

Govilon station had a staff of seven people. The single-storey building was situated on the Down platform. (GD)

When the line opened between Abergavenny and Brynmawr in 1862, this was the only stop until stations were built at Gilwern and Clydach. (AL)

Drawing by Michael Blackmore depicting Govilon station as it would have appeared in about 1950. (From *Portraits of the Past*: Blorenge Books)

Govilon station is the only one on this part of the line to have survived. It has now been converted into a private house and the track is a popular cycle route. (CB)

This gradient post was situated on the platform at Govilon station. (AL)

A modern sign at Govilon, which was erected when the track was turned into National Cycle Route 46 by Sustrans. (CB)

Gilwern station was opened in February 1863 and it became a halt in 1932. There was a timber station building on the Up platform and a wooden passenger shelter on the Down platform. Steps can be seen leading up to the road, which provided access from Gilwern village, half a mile away.

A 'Tuesdays-only' train at Gilwern station on the way to Merthyr, 22 July 1955. The platforms have survived and the track bed is part of National Cycle Route 46.

At this point of its journey the train leaves the Usk Valley and enters the Clydach Gorge, which is drained by the River Clydach, a short river that falls 900 feet (274 m) to its confluence with the Usk at Gilwern. The gorge is less than half a mile wide and under 4 miles long. It descends from 1,100 feet above sea level to 400 feet at Gilwern.

View into the Clydach Gorge from the railway line. (CB)

The Clydach Viaduct, built of Old Red Sandstone, is 312 feet long and 26 feet wide, and curves gracefully over the Nant Dyar. Note the signal box on the left, which was built in 1898 to control a private siding serving the limeworks and quarry on the right. (NL)

A view of the Clydach Viaduct and station building in August 2017. (CB)

From Cwm Dyar, below the viaduct, one can look up at this great structure and see the projections from the piers, which supported the wooden centring upon which the arches were constructed. It is also possible to see how the viaduct was widened on the upper side when the line was doubled in 1877. (CB)

A lone cyclist crossing John Gardner's beautiful viaduct on the present-day cycle route, which is a great way of enjoying the breathtaking beauty of the Clydach Gorge. (CB)

Overlooking the viaduct is Clydach Limeworks, which was established here to provide lime for the construction of the viaduct and Clydach Tunnel. The main bank of lime kilns was built when the line was doubled in 1877. The kilns ceased burning lime in 1930 but were used again during the Second World War when there was a high demand for lime for agricultural purposes. It was last burned here in 1955. (CB)

Clydach station with its staff in 1907. There were two platforms (which still survive) and the station building stands on the Up track. (GD)

Clydach station opened in 1863 and closed in January 1958. It is now a private house, so please note that there is no access along the old railway track to the tunnels. (CB)

The building on the right is the old station hotel, where people waiting for a train could enjoy some refreshment. It closed many years ago and is now a private dwelling. (CB)

Just up the road from the station is Nazareth Chapel (also known as Cuckoo Chapel), which used to operate a Gretna Green-type wedding service for eloping couples who arrived here by train. (CB)

At one time tourists used to get out at Clydach to visit the waterfalls. There used to be a placard at Clydach station describing it as having 'cascades, deep ravines, ponderous rocks, footpaths, seats, steps and a bridge leading to renowned springs. The whole area has been opened up as a health and pleasure resort'. (Old Postcard)

The line passed through Dinas Hill, which is crowned by an Iron Age fort.

A group of local people watch the last train pass through Clydach Tunnel in January 1958. The Up tunnel is 330 yards long and the Down is 302 yards long. There is a gradient of 1 in 38 and these tunnels had to be constructed because the locomotives could not negotiate the curves of Bailey's Tramroad. (GD)

The western portals of the Clydach Tunnels. The one on the right was made in 1877 when the line was doubled. (Drawing by Michael Blackmore, from *Portraits of the Past*: Blorenge Books)

A present-day view of the 1877 tunnel portal, which was taken in August 2017. The original portal on the left is hidden by trees. (CB)

Llanelly level crossing was kept by three generations of the Needs family over the years. Mrs Needs was the crossing keeper and when she died her daughter, Emma, at just fifteen years of age, became the official crossing keeper. In due course she married and as Mrs Jenkins retained the position for over fifty years, until her retirement in 1933. Her daughter, Mrs Evelyn Francis, then took over and remained in the position until the line closed. (GD)

A present-day view of the site of the Llanelly level crossing, with the railway line going to the right and the road to Llanelly Hill ascending on the left. (CB)

The line curving round past the high rockface on the side of Llanelly Hill. (NL)

The same view in August 2017. (CB)

An LMSR goods train hauled by a 0-8-4 tank locomotive seen climbing the 1 in 38 bank near Gelli Felin – picture by Oscar Elsden. (GD)

The same location photographed from the other side of the gorge. (CB)

The line then entered the Gelli Felin Tunnel, which is 325 yards long, is mostly masonry-lined, and runs on a 90 degree curve to emerge on a sharp left-hand curve. The northerly tunnel was the first to be built, being followed by the other one when the track was doubled in 1877. (NL)

This picture, taken in August 2017, shows how the tunnel entrances look now. The cycle path curving to the right follows the route of the old Bailey Tramroad, which could not be used for the railway because the curves were too sharp. (CB)

Gelli Felin Halt was established by the LMSR following a petition by local residents. It was opened with a grand ceremony on Wednesday, 6 September 1933. Two brick huts served as passenger shelters on each side of the track and they can still be seen. (NL)

Above: The same brick shelter in August 2017. (CB)

Left: A signal box, known as Gellavalin, was built on the Up line in 1898. It had disappeared by 1931. (GD)

The line now approaches Brynmawr, which is the highest town of its size in Britain, with most of the built-up area being at between 1,000 feet and 1,300 feet above sea level. It grew up in the nineteenth century as a centre for gathering raw materials for the nearby smelting industry, and by 1880 a town was well established here, with a population of about 7,000 people.

Brynmawr station looking west. Situated at a height of 1,160 feet above sea level, it was necessary for locomotives to take on extra water, having climbed no less than 1,000 feet over a distance of 8 miles. (GD)

Brynmawr station opened on 1 October 1862 and was located to the south of the town centre. The Brynmawr & Blaenavon Railway constructed a 4-mile line to Blaenavon, which opened for goods traffic on 1 November 1869 and to passengers on 1 January 1870. The extension southwards to Nantyglo opened in 1906 and was jointly worked by the Great Western and LNWR. Passenger services to Nantyglo were withdrawn on 30 April 1962 and the station finally closed on 4 November 1963 when its goods services were withdrawn. Brynmawr station is now the site of a small industrial estate. (GD)

Westward from Brynmawr, the line climbed by a final mile of 1 in 88 to its highest point, just under 1,200 feet at the east end of Beaufort Tunnel. This meant that travelling beyond Brynmawr in winter could be a very worrying undertaking, as snow was a serious threat at this altitude. At Christmas 1927, there were no less than fourteen locomotives snowbound at various points along the line. Forty passengers on one train were marooned for twelve hours. Snow was cleared from the line in 1947 by the use of two Gloster Whittle jet engines, which were supplied by the RAF and mounted on the railway to make a most ingenious snowplough!

Snowbound locomotives. (GD)

Beaufort station was situated in a small cutting, which gave it shelter from the elements. This was the point where passengers changed for Ebbw Vale and it was quite busy until 1925, there being a frequent daily service from here to Brynmawr. (GD)

Ex-GWR 0-6-0PT No. 6433 at Beaufort station (1,200 feet above sea level) in June 1955. Beaufort station had two platforms that were reached by steps leading down from the road bridge. The station was built of stone with an awning and a timber waiting room on the opposite platform. The site of the station was destroyed when the cutting was infilled. (GD)

Beaufort Viaduct, spanning the River Ebbw, was completed in August 1863. The seven-coach train in this picture virtually takes up the entire length of the structure. (GD)

At Trefil Halt the office and signal box was in one building. (NL)

The graceful 118-yard-long Blaen y Cwm Viaduct curves to the south over the River Sirhowy. It has nine 30-foot-span arches built in brick, while the remainder of the structure is limestone. It is situated at an altitude of 1,165 feet to the north of the small settlement of Nantybwch and was built in 1864 to a design by John Gardner. It has been given a Grade 2 listing and it was re-opened in 2008 to form part of National Cycle Route 46. (CB)

The Blaen y Cwm Viaduct, also known as Nine Arches, takes the line over the River Sirhowy. (CB)

Nantybwch station was opened on 1 March 1864 and was originally called Tredegar. It was later renamed Nantybwch and became a junction for the Sirhowy Valley line. It was situated in a desolate location and the platforms had no shelters, although the footbridge was covered. There were two platforms either side of a curving island platform and they were lit by gas lights. The Merthyr-bound platform incorporated a ticket office and porters' room. Signal box No. 1, on the island platform, was built in 1891. This station closed on 13 June 1960 with the withdrawal of the Sirhowy services, and the site is now under the A465. (NL)

Nantybwch signal box No. 2 is believed to have been built by the Rhymney Railway Company to control the goods siding. This picture was taken a year after the line closed. (GD)

The next stop was Rhymney Bridge station, where the line from Cardiff joined the MTA – a service withdrawn on 21 September 1953. It was a single-storey brick building with a covered bridge. When the A465 was built, the site of the station was covered by a roundabout. (NL)

An ICI ammonia train from Dowlais passing through Rhymney Bridge station. The signal box can be seen in the 'V' of the junction and behind it is the footbridge, which is covered to provide protection from the elements. (NL)

Dowlais High Street station was opened by the LNWR on 4 May 1885. It was a timber building situated on a curved embankment to the east of the town centre. (GD)

Ivor Junction's Brecon & Merthyr railway box. The line on the left is the B&M to Brecon and the line to the right is the LNWR to Penywern Junction. (GD)

The line now plunged into the double-track Morlais Tunnel, which is 1,037 yards long and descends towards Merthyr at a gradient of 1 in 60. At its deepest point, it is 80 feet below ground. John Gardner was in charge of this LNWR project and John Charles Mackay, the contractor, employed 800 men, who worked in relays day and night. They made rapid progress, completing the tunnel within two years. A date stone was inserted into the wall above the entrance but it is now covered with vegetation. This photograph was taken in August 2017. (CB)

One of three Grade 2 listed shafts, which were used during the excavation of the tunnel. Originally there were five of them and three were left for ventilation, but the other two were filled in. The earth was brought up each shaft in skips hauled by winding engines. As many as twenty-five skips an hour were raised during construction of the tunnel. (CB)

The exit portal of the Morlais Tunnel at Morlais Junction, August 2017. (CB)

The Morlais Tunnel Junction is where the B&M Railway's single line from Pontsticill came in on a sharp curve from the right. This junction marks the end of the LNWR double track from Abergavenny Junction, 19 miles away. On the right is the last ex-LNWR signal box on the line. (NL)

The section from Morlais Junction to Rhydcar Junction was jointly run with the BMR and was opened on 1 August 1868.

Due to objections made by the Crawshay family, the route taken by the BMR had to keep well clear of Cyfarthfa Castle by going down the west side of the Taff Fechan Valley. This involved a continuous descent of 1 in 45–50 and the need for the construction of two large stone viaducts at Pontsarn and Cefn Coed.

Descending continuously from Morlais Junction, the single-track line crossed a seven-arch stone viaduct at Pontsarn, carrying it 90 feet above the Taff Fechan Gorge.

Built of local limestone and 150 yards long, Pontsarn Viaduct was wide enough for a double track, but this was never laid. (GD)

The Pontsarn Viaduct is still in very good condition. (CB)

The line then passed under a stone bridge that carried the road to Talybont and reached Pontsarn station, which was opened in 1867 by the BMR. By 1873 there were twenty-one trains a day passing through this small station and this number increased the following year when the LNWR made an agreement for joint operation. It ceased to be staffed in 1934 and in the 1950s was renamed Pontsarn Halt.

This view of Pontsarn Joint station shows stationmaster Richard Hancock in the foreground. Other members of staff and passengers are awaiting the next train.

Pontsarn station is no longer there, but the platform remains, although it is very overgrown. The former track bed has been incorporated into the Taff Trail, which links Cardiff with Brecon and is used by both cyclists and walkers, providing a fascinating journey under one's own steam. (CB)

The Station Hotel at Cefn Coed, August 2017. (CB)

Cefn Coed station was on the right-hand (Up) side of the track. It was closed to passengers on 13 November 1961 and to goods traffic on 4 May 1964. (NL)

The detailed nameboard at Cefn Coed station instructed passengers to change there for the LMS line and vice versa. (GD)

The land occupied by the main station building and goods shed is now occupied by this block of flats. (CB)

The line then crossed the very impressive Cefn Coed Viaduct, which has fifteen arches and is 242 yards long. It was built by Messrs Savin and Ward from designs prepared by Alexander Sutherland and was completed in 1866 at a cost of £25,000. Built on a graceful curve, it stands 122 feet above the River Taff Fawr.

Now designated as a Grade 2 listed structure, this is the third largest stone viaduct in Wales and is a masterpiece of Victorian engineering.

The route of the line from the southern end of the viaduct has been destroyed by the A470 dual carriageway leading to Cardiff.

Originally the arches were to be built completely in stone, but on 17 February 1866 all 350 of the masons stopped work as they were against nineteen non-union masons being employed. After two months the union members gave in and resumed work on the old terms; however, after working just one day, half of them were discharged. On the following day one third of the remainder were paid off, as it had then been decided to have the arches built of brick. The arches of 40 feet span contain 800,000 bricks, which were obtained from brickworks near Hirwaun and Welshpool. (CB)

A view of the Cefn Coed Viaduct from the south, beside the Taf Fawr. (CB)

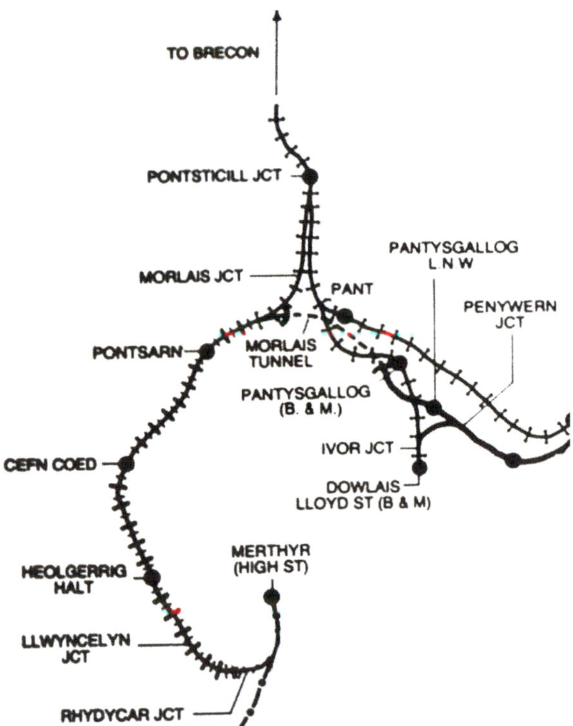

This map shows the descent route from Cefn Coed, which was continuously downhill at a gradient of 1 in 50 through Llwyncelyn Junction, and followed an anti-clockwise curve to reach Merthyr High Street station. The LNWR operated this line jointly with the BMR.

At last we arrive at Merthyr High Street station, which was built by the famous engineer Isambard Kingdom Brunel in 1853. At Merthyr, all five of the following railway companies – GWR, LNWR, BMR, TVR and the RR – made use of Brunel's Vale of Neath terminus for their passenger traffic. (GD)

On the right can be seen some remains of the Brunelian roof. The locomotive is a Class 2 Ivatt Tank with a train for Abergavenny. (NL)

A new Tesco superstore has been built on the site of High Street station, which Brunel had designed in the style of Paddington station – the Great Western terminal in London that he had developed earlier. At one time six lines ran through Merthyr High Street station, but they all closed through the 1950s and '60s, except for the Cardiff line. As a result this station was too large, and it was closed in the 1960s to be replaced by a very simple affair, which can be seen below. (CB)

5

CLOSURE OF THE ABERGAVENNY TO MERTHYR LINE

The importance of Abergavenny as a railway centre began to change when forty firemen were made redundant in one day. The decline continued until the First World War, when it halted for a while. After that the depression was even worse. Nationalisation followed and the South Wales division lost its independence. With it went the railway centre at Abergavenny, which became part of the Western Region of British Railways.

It was announced in 1957 that British Rail wished to close the Abergavenny to Merthyr line, and a meeting was held in the town by local people to prepare a case to fight this decision. Unfortunately, passenger and freight traffic on the line at that time was so small that closure was inevitable. It was duly announced in the *Merthyr Express*

This historic picture shows the last pay packets being brought to the loco sheds. In the background is the Union Road Bridge, which was later demolished to be replaced by a footbridge. The railway line is now a road. (AL)

and the *Abergavenny Chronicle* on 29 November 1957 that the line would close, thereby saving British Rail about £60,000 a year.

In January 1958 a special train arranged by the Stephenson Locomotive Society (Midland Area) to commemorate the sad closure of this remarkable line completed the journey from Abergavenny to Merthyr and back. It was driven by George Lewis, who had first started work in the sheds at Brecon Road in November 1911. He was assisted by fireman Derek Hinton and the train guard was Hubert James of Abergavenny.

The engine was boosted by No. 49121, a superheated 'D', driven by Mr F. Brown, whose grandfather was one of the first drivers to make the trip after the line opened in 1879. The fireman was Mr A. E. Baker.

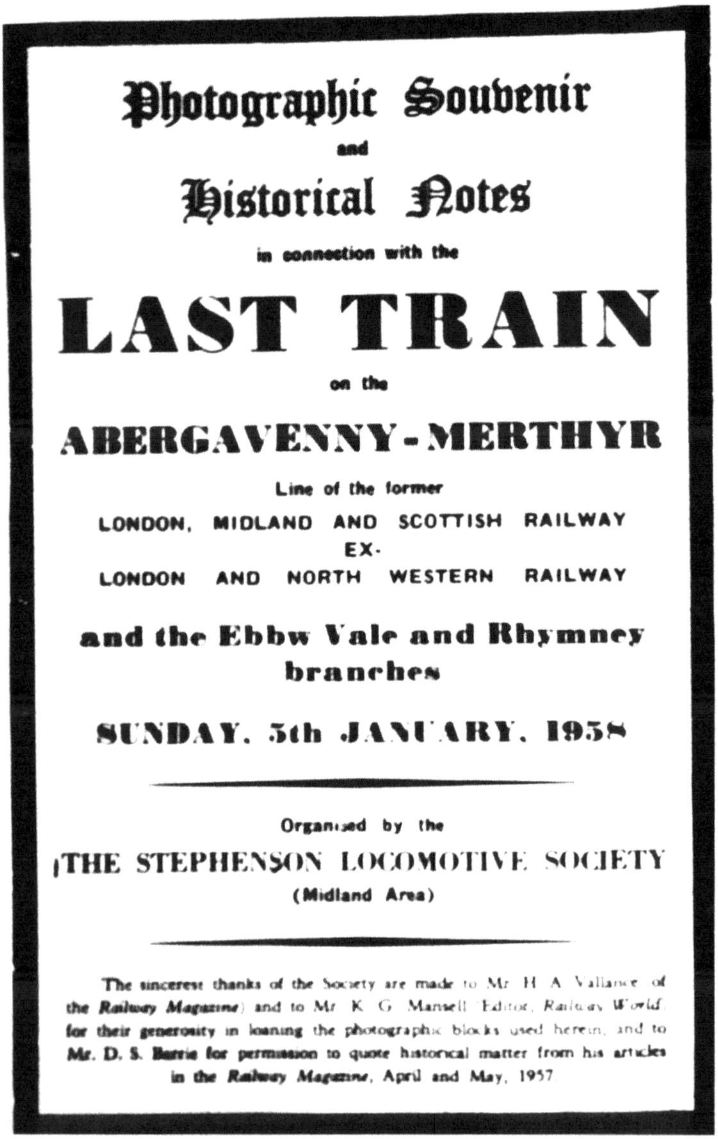

Photographic Souvenir
and
Historical Notes
in connection with the
LAST TRAIN
on the
ABERGAVENNY - MERTHYR
Line of the former
LONDON, MIDLAND AND SCOTTISH RAILWAY
EX-
LONDON AND NORTH WESTERN RAILWAY
and the Ebbw Vale and Rhymney branches
SUNDAY, 5th JANUARY, 1958

Organised by the
THE STEPHENSON LOCOMOTIVE SOCIETY
(Midland Area)

The sincerest thanks of the Society are made to Mr H A Vallance (of the *Railway Magazine*) and to Mr K G Mansell (Editor, *Railway World*) for their generosity in loaning the photographic blocks used herein, and to Mr. D. S. Barrie for permission to quote historical matter from his articles in the *Railway Magazine*, April and May, 1957

Copies of this souvenir programme were handed out to passengers at the start of their journey to Merthyr. It is now a collector's item and a treasured possession for some.

This picture shows the leading engine, 0-6-2 Webb Coal Tank No. 58926, and the second engine, 0-8-0 No. 49121, hauling the last passenger train on the Abergavenny to Merthyr line under the Hereford Road Bridge. (SB)

At Monmouth Road station, copies of a twelve-page souvenir programme were handed out to the travellers before the start of the five-hour trip to Merthyr and back again. On board were 250 members of the Stephenson Locomotive Society and many railway employees who were travelling on the line for the last time.

The train left at 12.45 p.m. and took thirty minutes to complete the climb up through the Clydach Gorge to Brynmawr, where, despite the cold day, huge crowds had gathered to say their farewell. In fact, large numbers of people gathered at all the stations and halts along the route, with everyone cheering and waving.

There was a brief stop at Nantybwch before the train proceeded to Rhymney Bridge, where sightseers lined the bridge and platform. Here, Mr T. A. Mountjoy, Newport's Running Maintenance Inspector, placed a laurel wreath on the smokebox door of the coal tank and doffed his trilby as a mark of respect to the old lady.

When the train returned from Merthyr, there was a 'whistle up' at every station and on the approach to Abergavenny there was a tremendous eruption of steam, with showers of sparks illuminating the night sky. Householders adjoining the line even switched their lights on and off in reply.

Engines and carriages were then moved away to be scrapped and railway employees were retired or transferred to other depots at Pontypool or Hereford. The Brecon Road yard remained as a feeder for coal merchants until April 1971. Six years later, the Brecon Road, Chapel Road and Pen y Pound railway bridges were demolished and a large area of former railway land was reclaimed in a Welsh Development Agency scheme to tidy up Abergavenny.

Enthusiasts at Brynmawr watching the last train to Merthyr pass through. Health and safety or risk assessment did not apply in those days! (NL)

The SLS Special on its return to Abergavenny Junction, 5 January 1958. (SB)

Brecon Road station was 'To Let' when this photo was taken. It was later demolished and a doctor's surgery now stands on the site. (NL)

Demolition of the iron viaduct spanning the River Usk, photographed in 1963. (AL)

The Union Road locomotive shed seen just before demolition. (NL)

Brecon Road station was in a very poor state before demolition. (NL)

A Memorial to the Railway People of Abergavenny

In November 2000, a bronze plaque was unveiled at Hatherleigh Place, just yards from the site of the local engine sheds at Union Road that once housed a large number of steam engines. It was unveiled by John Harvey, Mayor of Abergavenny, who said:

> Abergavenny had an unrivalled part in the Industrial Revolution with its ironworks, canals and railways. Our Principality can claim to be the first to have a steam locomotive run on rails and to have the first passenger carrying railway in the world.
>
> Our town's part in railway history is unchallenged, the LMS and the Great Western were both established here and the building of the Abergavenny to Merthyr Railway made Abergavenny the ideal venue for a day out.

The plaque was based on a drawing by local artist Michael Blackmore, whose two grandfathers had spent a lifetime working on the railways. The engine portrayed is a 0-6-2 Webb coal tank bearing the name of the LMS Company, but which originally belonged to the LNWR. The project cost about £1,400 and money was raised by selling limited editions of Michael Blackmore's original drawing of the steam engine that adorns the plaque.

On 10 September 2013, Coal Tank No. 1054 made a return visit to Abergavenny on a low loader transporter. It was then taken up to the Blaenavon & Pontypool Railway to

The inscription reads: 'This plaque is to commemorate the railway people of Abergavenny 1860–1960 and is near the local engine sheds, which once housed nearly 100 steam engines'.

Coal Tank No. 1054 comes home to Abergavenny. (PS)

participate in their annual Gala, in which they also had a Super D, and this enabled them to re-enact the last train as near to its original location as possible.

No. 1054 was built at the Crewe Locomotive Works of the LNWR in 1888 and it is the last surviving example of a class of 300 'Side Tank Coal Engines,' or 'Coal Tanks' as they became known. Intended for use on mineral and goods traffic, they proved equally suitable for local passenger trains. Under the ownership of the LMS Railway, No. 1054 became No. 7799 and later No. 58926 under British Railways. It was withdrawn from service in late 1958.

The engine was purchased for preservation in 1960, and was restored to its former LNWR livery. After temporary storage at Hedensford, No. 1054 was presented to the National Trust for display at its Industrial Railway Museum at Penrhyn Castle in North Wales. It was later placed into the care of the Bahamas Locomotive Society, whose volunteer members overhauled and restored it to working order at the Dinting Railway Centre in Derbyshire.

It underwent a comprehensive overhaul after a successful bid to the Heritage Lottery Fund in 2004, and this was completed in 2011. The Bahamas Locomotive Society continue to care for it at their museum, Ingrow Loco, on the Keighley & Worth Valley Railway.

A present-day autumn view of the line just before the Gelli Felen Tunnels. (CB)

Some people assume that the MTA Railway was closed by Dr Beeching, but it was shut down about four years before his now infamous report was published. The Beeching Report resulted in the devastation of Britain's extensive network of railways, reducing the total mileage from 23,000 to barely 10,000 and causing great hardship for people living in remote places.

The surviving section of the MTA in the Clydach Gorge is very beautiful now that nature has taken over, with ever-changing colours through the seasons. But Crawshay Bailey, chairman of the MTA Company, would no doubt be very unhappy if he could see it now, and it is important to remember that the construction of this railway was only achieved by his foresight and determination.

A cycle path now starts from the Old Crossing car park at Llanfoist and follows the line of the former MTA Railway for 8 miles up through the Clydach Gorge to Brynmawr. It is part of the National Cycle Network created by the sustainable transport charity Sustrans and was officially opened by the Welsh Assembly Heritage Minister Alun Ffred Jones. It had taken more than two decades to complete and has proved an excellent facility for both cyclists and walkers, who are able to appreciate the skill of the Victorian engineers who built it in such a short time.

Bibliography

Books

Barber, C. & Blackmore, M., *Portraits of the Past*, (1996).
Edge, D., *Abergavenny to Merthyr*, (2002).
Hall, M., *Lost Railways of South Wales*, (2009).
Jones, B. G. & Dunstone, D., *The Origins of the LMS in South Wales*, (1999).
Murray, J., *A Handbook for Travellers in South Wales*, (1870).
Page, J., *Forgotten Railways*, (1988).
Rattenbury, G., *Tramroads of the Brecknock & Abergavenny Railway*, (1980).
Reed, M. C., *The London & North Western Railway*, (1996).
Tasker W. W., *The Merthyr, Tredegar & Abergavenny Railway*, (1986).

Newspapers

Abergavenny Chronicle, (1957–1959).
Hereford Times, (1859–1860).
Merthyr Express, (1957–1958).